MW01644754

Complete Horoscope Cancer 2020

Monthly astrological forecasts for 2020

TATIANA BORSCH

CONTENTS

General Forecast For Cancer

Bringing back something or someone from your past will not lead anywhere. In the first half of the year everything seems rosy enough, but in the second half of the year you finally see cold, hard reality. This is true both in working and romantic relationships.

Business. 2020 might be controversial professionally. The beginning of the year is quite favourable and there may be co-operation with people you already know. They might be your former partners, some old friends or even an old flame and everything will go smoothly at the beginning.

However, the second half of the year will be more difficult and demanding. It will turn out that your colleagues have a different vision regarding the development of the business and its future. It is also possible that you will have differing opinions about investments and the contribution of each participant. Misunderstandings, arguments and possible distribution of joint assets may result. You should also understand that your position looks weak and it might be you who has to back down.

In a different scenario, you might have problems with authorities who put obstacles in front of you.

Some changes will take place for clerical workers, and these might turn out to be quite painful. As a result, many of your sign may need to think about other ways to apply their talents. The most difficult period in this respect will be from June to December.

Co-operation with colleagues from other cities or overseas is not stable; some projects are successful while others are not. This requires your constant attention and control.

Those who have legal problems might find themselves in a serious situation, especially when your lawyers are either slow or incompetent or both.

Money. This is a heck of a year financially. The financial situation is up and down. Closer to December you will have to admit that you actually are in the red. If you are lucky, you will break even.

Love and family. For many Cancerians, the main battles of 2020 will take place within the family. It is especially serious for those couples who have already had some troubles. It is not unlikely that an old love will come back into circulation or that your ex-spouse might want reconciliation; you might even decide to give your relationship with them another chance. At the beginning of the year all is smooth, but in the second half of the year it will become clear that you have again been caught in the same old trap. It is hard to understand who is to blame, but that doesn't really matter; the main thing is that it did not work out.

If spouses are co-owners of business or property, it will make the situation even more complicated. Beware! It is possible that in the case of a break-up you will be left with nothing as your now ex-partner is determined and will not budge an inch regarding money.

Strong couples, with the help of their love and wisdom, will be able to overcome all obstacles together.

Health. Your energy levels are not good in 2020 and you might regularly suffer from apathy and fatigue. This will be more evident in the second half of the year which will turn out to be a considerably difficult period.

In January your plans receive support and your dreams might come true. This may be hard to believe this as things have not been good for a while, but the stars are on your side now and you should start to believe in your coming good fortune.

Business. January is a time for active communication and co-operation. You might be surrounded by new partners, former colleagues, and those with power and money; their support will help you to resolve any past problems and make for a better future. This is true for all Cancerians, but mainly for those who have outstanding legal issues or who face the consequences of the actions of government institutions. The time has come to fix these problems and you can ask your partners and colleagues for help without hesitation as you will be heard and understood correctly.

Your relations with colleagues from other cities and overseas are developing well. You might have a lucrative business trip, meet new partners or sign new contracts that give the future a bright outlook.

Money. Although your professional competence is growing, your financial situation will not change in the first twenty days of January.

The situation will improve after the new moon on January 24th when you can rely on the support of your business partners or close friends and relatives. The financial situation might change for the better in the last ten days of the month or in February.

Love and family. January is a time for romance. Single people will meet somebody interesting and there is a good chance that this affair will grow into marriage. Your current relationship might improve. Couples who have split up as a result of arguments, misunderstandings or distance might reconsider and begin thinking about getting back together. Go for it! You should remember that this is a unique opportunity to change your life and that you will not have such a possibility in the second part of the year.

Trips that you have planned for January will be successful. Every evening of this romantic month is perfect for dating or for heart-to-heart talks.

The active period for relationships in January is from the 1st to the 24th.

The last ten days of this month are better for tranquil reflection on the events; it is worth having a break from people and fresh experiences.

Health. Your energy levels are quite high in the first twenty days of the month, and you should not worry about your health.

Nevertheless, it is always wise to take care of your health and the stars recommend paying extra attention to your digestive system. After the New moon, on the 24th of January, your energy levels will fall dramatically, and so you should take extra care of yourself.

Being wise and open minded may open new doors for you; especially if you remember the old saying, 'no man is an island'.

Business. The first half of the month is a reasonable and quite predictable period. You can expect support from your business partners and to meet new people who may turn out to be both interesting and quite powerful. Entrepreneurs and managers will be busy discussing financial plans, such as capital and other financial injections into a joint business; these questions will definitely be solved, but only after much debate.

Clerical workers will have a quiet period with neither achievements nor troubles. Many of your birth sign will want to take a break and go to the seaside to enjoy some sunny weather. Those who stay at work should be attentive to their duties, especially during the second half of the month.

During this period, you might be faced with business difficulties such as paperwork and red tape.

Those who have legal problems should be extra careful with documentation. It is also worth paying more attention to the work of your lawyers; this will help you to avoid many problems either now or in future. Your relations with colleagues from other cities and overseas are developing well, although in the second half of the month you should be cautious and pay more attention to detail.

Money. The financial situation is generally stable, but this mainly concerns the finances of your business rather than your own income. You might receive the reimbursement of an old debt or get a loan on easy terms.

You might have to deal with numerous costs, but these are organizational costs and so they are expected. Those in romantic relationships can expect support from a more prosperous partner.

Love and family. Everything is well and quiet in your personal life. Married couples who have recently made up can enjoy a happy family life or perhaps go on a second honeymoon somewhere far from home.

Long-term lovers will have a similar period in their lives. Single people might see an old friend from a new angle - you will be surprised that you hadn't noticed such a diamond right there next to you. Even if you have doubts in the second half of the month, you should not worry - love is in the air.

Health. Your energy levels are not high in the first twenty days of February and you might feel lethargic, tired and lazy.

You can expect a burst of energy after the new moon on the 24th of February and you will feel happier, more cheerful and confident after this.

'All that is new is really just something old that has been overlooked' – this sentiment is very appropriate for March and applies, to both work and love.

Business. In the first ten days of March, entrepreneurs and managers will continue to have the same problems that they had in February. All activities take a very long time and there are constant delays. ,Everything will begin to work out better in the second half of the month, however, and you will finally start to see the light at the end of the tunnel. This light becomes brighter each day and eventually you will hit the bull's eye.

Relations with your colleagues from other cities and overseas will become more important and there is a strong possibility of a business trip. If you have been discussing future co-operation with your partners, now is the moment of truth – you will see what you have or have not achieved. Your business partners will play a very important role in all the activities of the month and their influence on your business will be positive.

The best time for all professional events is the last ten days of the month - try to plan all the most important activities for this period.

One more piece of advice – you should be cautious with new people who appear in your life between the 17th of February and the 10th of March for they will turn out to be unreliable and you would be better off not trusting them. –This is true both for work and love.

Money. The financial situation is stable. In March the largest amounts of money might come in on the 6th, 7th, 15th, 16th and the 26th to the 28th.

Love and family. Things are going well in your personal life. Both married couples and lovers will be in harmony with each other this month and will probably plan a romantic trip. ,

Single people might dive into an exciting romantic relationship, but the stars advise that you bear in mind the difficult period from the 17th of February to the 10th of March. You will soon be disappointed by these people if you cannot trust them; those who you meet later will better fulfil your expectations. The stars therefore recommend that you dress up and socialise more in the second half of the month.

Health. In March your energy levels are quite high and there is no need to worry about your health.

April is like being in your own thriller – full of tension, shady backroom deals and constant conflict. Emotions run high and this is true for both work and for love.

Business. There are plenty of unexpected changes in the professional sphere. It is possible that you will have serious disagreements with business partners who see the development of the business differently from you. Furthermore, there are likely to be unexpected financial problems not only with your partners but with other key people.

You should be cautious because your partner's position is stronger and if you fall out with them you might be shooting yourself in the foot. You need to be more reserved and tactful; no matter how hard it might seem at times. You should consider all possibilities and try to steadily unravel the tangle. Looking further forward, we can say that most of the problems will be solved at the end of April and beginning of May.

Money. Money is another aspect of your life where problems are possible in April. You should be extra careful between the 6th of April and the 17th of April when the chances of financial loss are quite high.

During this period, it is possible to be faced with theft and other adverse circumstances related not only to money but to other material assets. Those who work in finance such as brokers, accountants and bank staff should be especially cautious.

If you have any debt you should bear in mind that you might be faced with some very tough demands this month.

Love and family. The situation in your personal life is also complicated. All your hopes for a future spent together do not look so promising now. Do not jump to conclusions! You need time to understand how much you need one another, and April is not the best time for making big decisions.

Emotions run high and any conversations may end up with arguments and outbursts of anger. If you are connected to each other not only romantically and by family, but also professionally, your situation will be more complicated still. If this is true for you, you should not allow yourself to be blown away by emotion but to remain patient and grounded. The problems will not last forever and every cloud indeed has a silver lining. At the end of April or the beginning of May, the situation is likely to improve. If it does not, you will find comfort in that you did everything possible.

Health. Your energy levels are not high this month. There is an especially unfavourable period from the 6th of April to the 15th of April when there is a strong possibility of unexpected illness, injury and accident.

It is unlikely that you will be alone this month. At the moment you are in-demand and extremely popular among your acquaintances, friends and partners.

Business. The first half of May is really successful period for meetings, negotiations and discussions of future plans. Even while on holiday, you will continue running your business in an 'online' way. Friends and patrons will be well-disposed towards you and will help you in any way they can. The trips you planned for this period will be successful.

The second half of May is more complicated. Entrepreneurs and managers of different levels should prepare for inspections that will more than likely drag on and cause a number of problems.

In a different scenario, relationships with colleagues from other cities and overseas will get more complicated. Long-distance business partners might act rudely; their actions could harm any budding co-operation.

Furthermore, entrepreneurs and clerical workers should be aware that any ugly errors in their work might be revealed closer to the end of the month.

Money. The financial situation is not quite stable this month. There will be lots of expenses while your income will be low. You might even have empty pockets at the end of the month. The stars recommend being more careful with money, and especially in the second half of the month. This period is not a good one for spending or investing money.

Love and family. The first half of May is good for resting and spending time with friends and like-minded people. Do not be shy in expressing your love for your close friends and family members - this will make them happy. During this period, relations between spouses and lovers are harmonious. You might spend time together with your partner on a holiday, having parties, making new friends and high-up contacts.

During the second half of the month the situation will change slightly for the worse as a result of undesirable information, gossip and rumours. This will have an impact on both your personal and professional relationships.

During this period, disagreements with relatives are possible and it is likely that these misunderstandings will happen with your in-laws. In all the difficult situations in this period, you should try to stay calm and sensible, no matter how difficult it might be at times.

Health. Those who fortunately escape any personal and professional troubles might unfortunately have problems with their health. Remember that the period from the 14th to the 31st of May is not lucky. It is possible that you will have new problems with your health or a recurrence of an old disease.

Drivers should be extra cautious.

This month you will be burdened with a number of problems that seem insoluble at first. As they say, 'a journey of thousand miles begins with a single step' - this so very true for you!

Business. Most of the month is not very lucky. People involved in business will be faced with many misfortunes that might damage their reputation and undermine their positions. There is the possibility of undergoing inspections or the resurfacing of old legal problems.

The behaviour of partners from other cities or overseas might be not exactly friendly or correct and co-operation might go wrong for some time to come. You will need lots of time and an incredible effort to stabilize the situation. So, if you can bear the serious tensions of this month, you will succeed! Don't get yourself down because of possible worrying news - it is unlikely to be completely true and the situation might not, in reality, be that bad.

Clerical workers should take a break from work and deal with family or health matters. There is unlikely to be any progress at work, but problems, conflicts and clandestine deals are quite possible. The stars recommend listening rather than speaking because you might be misunderstood.

Money. The situation with money is quite ambiguous and complicated. You should try to cut down on your expenses and those of your family members. This situation will last for a few months but you can then expect a more positive period.

Love and family. Problems in your personal life are also possible. You should remember that some unpleasant secrets might be revealed this month that cause complications in the relationships with your partner and in-laws - conflicts are possible for the whole month. During this period, you should remember that you are very vulnerable, and people tend to see your weaknesses rather than your strengths.

Furthermore, being unable to concentrate and not being in the right place at the right time might lead to some cruel and unpleasant jokes being played on you.

To cut a long story short, June is hardly your finest hour and so you need to be more flexible, diplomatic and modest.

Health. Those lucky enough to escape personal and professional misfortune might have problems with health. It is possible that you will come down with the recurrence of an old disease or have new problems with your health. Also, you should be more cautious while travelling and driving as the possibility of accidents and unpleasant events is quite high this month.

The stars recommend cancelling long-distance trips because they will cause nothing but problems.

Buckle up your armour! The possibility of battle is quite high this month!

Business. A very difficult and combative month is ahead of you. Entrepreneurs will be faced with complicated negotiations where the main dispute might be mutual business interests, money or large property. The stars strongly advise you not to rush into things between the 1st and the 14th of July, no matter how much pressure you are under from circumstances and deadlines. Making haste will be your mistake so don't be nervous and flustered but rather consider all the possibilities rationally. In the case of legal problems, you should involve responsible and reliable specialists. You should also remember that your opponents' positions are quite stable and so you are unlikely to solve the problem peacefully. It is possible that you will have to walk many roads and study a lot of paperwork to defend your property.

Those who have relationships with colleagues from other cities and overseas will also face a number of problems. It might be difficult to reach out to your foreign partners, so be patient and try to solve your problems calmly. You should not expect any help with your issues between the 1st and the 15th of July as this time looks very unfavorable. Some problems are likely to be sorted closer to the end of July, others in August.

Money. Financially, the first twenty days of July look unstable and unclear. Only at the end of the month might you expect good money. You should be careful with your money and cut down on your expenses - this will help you to avoid many problems both now and in the future.

Love and family. Those who have long-standing problems in their personal life will undergo another series of property fights where your spouse or long-term partner is very confident and even aggressive. It is possible that you will have to take a serious decision in July – whether to stay together or to part and travel your own path. In many cases the second variant is more probable. If you are engaged in business together, the situation will be worse and you can expect a long battle over the partition of your business. The chances of getting what your want are small and so you should try to compromise and learn to come to agreement with your partner; no matter how hard it might be at times.

Health. Your energy levels are not high this month. Don't forget that a good night's sleep and walks in the countryside are very useful when trying to sort out your feelings and emotions.

The last month of summer brings significant improvement to your work and personal life. You will be able to get your own way and to achieve the desired results.

Business. A complicated situation with partners will improve, at least partly. We cannot talk about a complete resolution of the argument at the moment - the future proves this - but you can still obtain some form of compensation this month and you take use this opportunity.

Your relationships with colleagues from other cities and overseas are developing well and you might have a trip where you could meet new partners towards the end of the month.

Clerical workers will continue to face changes at work, and this will turn out to be a long-term situation.

If you feel like changing jobs, it is better to successfully negotiate a decent package and do so now - it is unlikely to be possible come the fall.

Money. Many of your birth sign will observe, with some satisfaction, an improvement in their financial situation by the end of the month. The possible reasons are repaid debts, earnings at work and other payments.

You will not have many expenses in August and they all will be sensible and predictable.

Love and family. The situation in your personal life will improve slightly. There is unfortunately no suggestion of making-up completely; lovers and spouses in troubled relationships are still at each other's throats, but the number of incidents will reduce. The influence of Venus, who comes into your sign on the 7th of August, means you are more tactful and reasonably minded than your partner.

In many families, relatives will act as peacemakers and mediators for warring spouses not only in August but also in September.

Health. Your energy levels are not high this month. You need to take a break from your struggles and have some rest; this should be possible in the last ten days of August and at the beginning of September.

SEPTEMBER

September is quite a frustrating month. On the one hand, you are very active and likely to do many things. On the other hand, you are unlikely to achieve your main goals. This in no way means that you should give up, however.

Business. The main achievement this month is the development of partnerships with your colleagues from other cities and overseas. With the assistance of both new and existing contacts, you might be able to settle a recent dispute you have had with some of your partners.

As the problem is so complex, you will not be able to completely resolve it this month and it is very possible that the current situation drags on into the future. Nevertheless, peaceful negotiations are possible, and you should make full use of this opportunity. The old saying, 'make love, not war' is always true and especially so for you now.

Clerical workers might witness a changing situation at work. It might be a change of management, a reorganisation or even the shuttering of the business. You should pay attention to all events because the changes will come to affect your own interests in due time. If the worst comes to the worst, you might try to find a different outlet for your talents.

Money. The financial situation will improve slightly; your income will increase and this will allow you to be more confident and optimistic about the future. The approximate dates for receiving good money this month are the 4th, 5th, 14th, 15th, 22nd, 23rd, 28th and 29th.

Love and family. The situation in your personal life will become calmer and more even. Although relatives will somehow manage to reconcile the conflict between spouses, the main underlying reason for the misunderstandings, either real estate or other property, remains. If spouses are involved in business together, the situation will only worsen.

In other words, you will have a multitude of problems this month and you will have to navigate them carefully in order for the situation not to become terminal. If you do actually split up, there is a strong possibility of the worst happening. If you are reading this well in advance, you should try to safeguard your situation as it might become difficult to do so later.

Relationships with your relatives are strengthening. Indeed, you might meet your relatives from a different city or abroad - maybe you will travel to them or they will travel to you.

The situation between lovers will improve and a possible journey together will make the relationship stronger.

Health. Your energy levels are quite high this month and there is no need to worry about your health.

There might be times when it seems that peace is impossible and there is no path to victory - the position of the stars shows exactly this. Try to keep your head above water and remember that you are quite vulnerable at the moment.

Business. Confrontation with partners will seriously intensify and there will be attempts to sabotage your business or to break it up; this is actually the same thing. The position of your opponents is really strong, and it seems you have no means of countering them. The only thing that you can do at the moment is to involve some competent lawyers and just play for time. The situation will improve a little by the end of the year, however, and it will be easier for you to stand your ground then.

Clerical workers continue to face changes at work, and it may even come to the question of dismissal this month.

Your relationships with colleagues from other cities or overseas develop well and this is the only aspect of your activities that looks quite promising. In the case of serious problems, it might be wise to go somewhere, at least for the time being.

Money. The financial situation looks quite uncertain although your income and expenses are quite sensible and predictable.

Love and family. If your interests center on your personal life, you might find yourself in a rather unpleasant situation even here. The question on the agenda is a breakdown in relations and the situation might be really serious this time. The reason for the conflicts might be real estate or, worse, a joint business. Although the influence of relatives might smooth the situation over to some extent, it is unlikely to resolve it completely. You should be circumspect as the risk of being left with nothing is very high at the moment.

Health. Your energy levels are not high this month and your stressful environment might lead to serious health problems. In such a situation, the astrologer can only advise sleeping well and eating properly at regular times.

November will be stressful and turbulent. Any emotional outbursts in the middle of the month need to be controlled; otherwise you will be left celebrating your successes on your own.

Business. The problems of recent months are still a priority and again the question is over disagreements with partners or over the division of a joint business. Although none of this is new to you, the situation will improve somewhat this month with the help of lawyers, friends, old friends or close relatives who act as mediators.

Your relationship with colleagues from faraway will be noticeably revitalized and you might have a successful journey.

Nevertheless, the problem with some high-ranking officials might continue and it is unlikely that you will be able to completely resolve it in the near future; December looks much better in this respect and so it makes sense to wait.

Clerical workers are likely to face some major changes at work that will only be completely settled next month - there is no point in trying to change anything at the moment or addressing management with any requests. During this quite complicated month you should not pressure people too much but try to make your point in a less obtrusive manner as only then will you be heard and understood.

Money. November does not look very promising financially. Your expenses will increase due to work or to problems in your personal life.

Love and family. Complications in your family life drag on and again the reason is joint property - more than likely residential. However, the situation will improve in November and this time children might be the mediators; their influence on your partner will soften any hostile sentiment and allow you to revisit some disputed issues.

Lovers might go on a journey together that refreshes and improves their relationship.

Happy couples will spend lots of time with their children and this will make them happy.

Health. Your energy levels are quite high this month and you should not worry about your health. November is an excellent time to go to the theatre or a museum, to travel a long or short distance or just to have a stroll outside.

You have a good chance to improve your financial and professional standing in December. The transition of Jupiter and Saturn allows you to draw a line under the problems that ended all your previous hopes.

Business. This month is a good one professionally and, by fixing old problems with opponents, you will be able to bring about a bright and positive change to your business.

Legal questions that have been poisoning your life for a long time will be sorted out this month. Although things may not develop in quite the way in which you had planned or dreamed, the story is not yet finished - this is a positive. You will have the chance to worry not about the past but about future business and future work. As the changes are unlikely to happen all at once, however, you will at least have the time to consider and to plan your actions.

Clerical workers will acquit themselves well, but the idea of changing jobs is still in the air and it is certain to happen in the near future.

Money. The financial situation improves to some extent, but you cannot yet call it stable - you need to be thrifty and think everything over a few times before investing any money.

Love and family. Everything becomes quiet in your personal life. This is especially true for spouses going through a divorce and those now set on a divorce settlement; it is a time for licking your wounds and totaling your gains and losses. There is a long year ahead when you will have to get used to living in an unfamiliar way or to being single. If you do find yourself in such a difficult and uncomfortable situation, do not be upset because after 2021 has finished you will come to a new period of your life that is brighter; more exciting and more positive. So, you have time to put your affairs, thoughts and feelings in order.

Happily married couples will start to consider moving to a new place; be it a new flat or a new house and this might well come to pass at some point in 2021.

Children make you happy and might even become the bridge between hostile spouses in families with problems.

Health. Your energy levels are not high this month so take good care of yourself and keep everything within its limits.

Zodiac connections and us - a guide to compatibility

Often, when we meet a person, we get a feeling that they are good and we take an instant liking to them. Another person, however, gives us immediate feelings of distrust, fear and hostility. Is there an astrological reason why people say that 'the first impression is the most accurate'? How can we detect those who will bring us nothing but trouble and unhappiness?

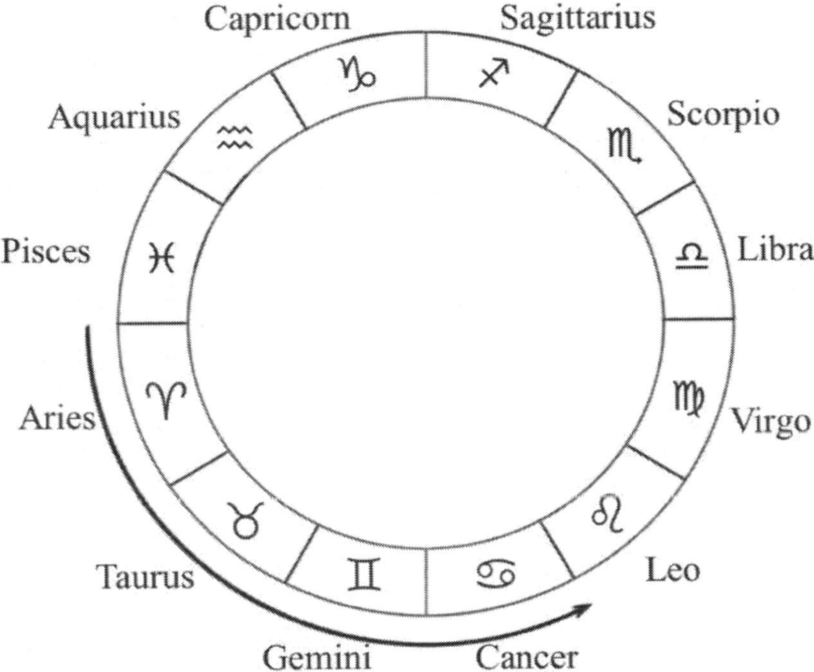

Without going too deeply into astrological subtleties unfamiliar to some readers, it is possible to determine the traits according to which friendship, love or business relationships will develop.

Let's begin with problematic relationships - our most difficult are with our 8th sign. For example, for Aries the 8th sign is Scorpio, for Taurus it is Sagittarius and so on. Finding your 8th sign is easy; assume your own sign to be first (see above Figure) and then move eight signs counter clockwise around the Zodiac circle. This is also how the other signs (fourth, ninth and so on) that we mention are to be found.

Ancient astrologers variously referred to the 8th sign as the symbol of death, of destruction, of fated love or unfathomable attraction. In astrological terms, this pair is called 'master and slave' or 'boa constrictor and rabbit', with the role of 'master' or 'boa constrictor' being played by our 8th sign.

This relationship is especially difficult for politicians and business people. We can take the example of a recent political confrontation in the USA. Hilary Clinton is a Scorpio while Donald Trump is a Gemini - her 8th sign. Even though many were certain that Clinton would be elected President, she lost.

To take another example, Hitler was a Taurus and his opponents – Stalin and Churchill - were both of his 8th sign, Sagittarius. The result of their confrontation is well known. Interestingly, the Russian Marshals who dealt crushing military blows to Hitler and so helped end the Third Reich - Konstantin Rokossovsky and Georgy Zhukov - were also Sagittarian, Hitler's 8th sign.

In another historical illustration, Lenin was also a Taurus. Stalin was of Lenin's 8th sign and was ultimately responsible for the downfall and possibly death of his one-time comrade-in-arms.

Business ties with those of our 8th sign are hazardous as they ultimately lead to stress and loss; both financial and moral. So, do not tangle with your 8th sign and never fight with it - your chances of winning are remote! Such relationships are very interesting in terms of love and romance, however. We are magnetically attracted to our 8th sign and even though it may be very intense physically, it is very difficult for family life; 'Feeling bad when together, feeling worse when apart'.

As an example, let us take the famous lovers - George Sand who was Cancer and Alfred de Musset who was Sagittarius. Cancer is the 8th sign for

Sagittarius, and the story of their crazy two-year love affair was the subject of much attention throughout France. Critics and writers were divided into 'Mussulist' and 'Sandist' camps; they debated fiercely about who was to blame for the sad ending to their love story - him or her. It's hard to imagine the energy needed to captivate the public for so long, but that energy was destructive for the couple. Passion raged in their hearts, but neither of them was able to comprehend their situation.

Georges Sand wrote to Musset, "I don't love you anymore, and I will always adore you. I don't want you anymore, and I can't do without you. It seems that nothing but a heavenly lightning strike can heal me by destroying me. Good-bye! Stay or go, but don't say that I am not suffering. This is the only thing that can make me suffer even more, my love, my life, my blood! Go away, but kill me, leaving." Musset replied only in brief, but its power surpassed Sand's tirade, "When you embraced me, I felt something that is still bothering me, making it impossible for me to approach another woman." These two people loved each other passionately and for two years lived together in a powder keg of passion, hatred and treachery.

When someone enters into a romantic liaison with their 8th sign, there will be no peace; indeed, these relationships are very attractive to those who enjoy the edgy, the borderline and, in the Dostoevsky style, the melodramatic. The first to lose interest in the relationship is, as a rule, the 8th sign.

If, by turn of fate, our child is born under our 8th sign, they will be very different from us and, in some ways, not live up to our expectations. It may be best to let them choose their own path.

In business and political relationships, the combination with our 12th sign is also a complicated one.

We can take two political examples. Angela Merkel is a Cancer while Donald Trump is a Gemini - her 12th sign. This is why their relations are strained and complicated and we can even perhaps assume that the American president will achieve his political goals at her expense. Boris Yeltsin (Aquarius) was the 12th sign to Mikhail Gorbachev (Pisces) and it was Yeltsin who managed to dethrone the champion of Perestroika.

Even ancient astrologers noticed that our relationships with our 12th signs can never develop evenly; it is one of the most curious and problematic combinations. They are our hidden enemies and they seem to be digging a hole for us; they ingratiate themselves with us, discover our innermost secrets. As a result, we become bewildered and make mistakes when we deal with them. Among the Roman emperors murdered by members of their entourage, there was an interesting pattern - all the murderers were the 12th sign of the murdered.

We can also see this pernicious effect in Russian history: the German princess Alexandra (Gemini) married the last Russian Tsar Nicholas II (Taurus) - he was her 12th sign and brought her a tragic death. The wicked genius Grigory Rasputin (Cancer) made friends with Tsarina Alexandra, who was his 12th sign, and was murdered as a result of their odd friendship. The weakness of Nicholas II was exposed, and his authority reduced after the death of the economic and social reformer Pyotr Stolypin, who was his 12th sign. Thus, we see a chain of people whose downfall was brought about by their 12th sign.

So, it makes sense to be cautious of your 12th sign, especially if you have business ties. Usually, these people know much more about us than we want them to and they will often reveal our secrets for personal gain if it suits them. However, the outset of these relationships is, as a rule, quite normal - sometimes the two people will be friends, but sooner or later one will betray the other one or divulge a secret; inadvertently or not.

In terms of romantic relationships, our 12th sign is gentle, they take care of us and are tender towards us. They know our weaknesses well but accept them with understanding. It is they who guide us, although sometimes almost imperceptibly. Sexual attraction is usually strong.
For example, Meghan Markle is a Leo, the 12th sign for Prince Harry, who is a Virgo. Despite Queen Elizabeth II being lukewarm about the match, Harry's love was so strong that they did marry.

If a child is our 12th sign, it later becomes clear that they know all our secrets, even those that they are not supposed to know. It is very difficult to control them as they do everything in their own way.
Relations with our 7th sign are also interesting. They are like our opposite; they have something to learn from us while we, in turn, have something to learn from them. This combination, in business and personal relationships, can be very positive and stimulating provided that both partners

are quite intelligent and have high moral standards but if not, constant misunderstandings and challenges follow. Marriage or co-operation with the 7th sign can only exist as the union of two fully-fledged individuals and in this case love, significant business achievements and social success are possible.

However, the combination can be not only interesting, but also quite complicated.

An example is Angelina Jolie, a Gemini, and Brad Pitt, a Sagittarius. This is a typical bond with a 7th sign - it's lively and interesting, but rather stressful. Although such a couple may quarrel and even part from time to time, never do they lose interest in each other.

This may be why this combination is more stable in middle-age when there is an understanding of the true nature of marriage and partnership. In global, political terms, this suggests a state of eternal tension - a cold war - for example between Yeltsin (Aquarius) and Bill Clinton (Leo).

Relations with our 9th sign are very good; they are our teacher and advisor - one who reveals things we are unaware of and our relationships with them very often involve travel or re-location. The combination can lead to spiritual growth and can be beneficial in terms of business.

Although, for example, Trump and Putin are political opponents, they can come to an understanding and even feel a certain sympathy for each other because Putin is a Libra while Trump is a Gemini, his 9th sign.

This union is also quite harmonious for conjugal and romantic relationships.

We treat our 3rd sign somewhat condescendingly. They are like our younger siblings; we teach them and expect them to listen attentively. Our younger brothers and sisters are more often than not born under this sign. In terms of personal and sexual relationships, the union is not very inspiring and can end quickly, although this is not always the case. In terms of business, it is fairly average as it often connects partners from different cities or countries.

We treat our 5th sign as a child and we must take care of them accordingly. The combination is not very good for business, however, since our 5th sign triumphs over us in terms of connections and finances, and thereby gives us very little in return save for love or sympathy. However, they are very good for family and romantic relationships, especially if the 5th sign is female. If a child is born as a 5th sign to their parents, their relationship will be a mutually smooth, loving and understanding one that lasts a lifetime.

Our 10th sign is a born leader. Depending on the spiritual level of those involved, both pleasant and tense relations are possible; the relationship is often mutually beneficial in the good times but mutually disruptive in the bad times. In family relations, our 10th sign always tries to lead and will do so according to their intelligence and upbringing.

Our 4th sign protects our home and can act as a sponsor to strengthen our financial or moral positions. Their advice should be heeded in all cases as it can be very effective, albeit very unobtrusive. If a woman takes this role, the relationship can be long and romantic, since all the spouse's wishes are usually met one way or another. Sometimes, such couples achieve great social success; for instance, Hilary Clinton, a Scorpio is the 4th sign to Bill Clinton, a Leo. On the other hand, if the husband is the 4th sign for his wife, he tends to be henpecked. There is often a strong sexual attraction. Our 4th sign can improve our living conditions and care for us in a parental way. If a child is our 4th sign, they are close to us and support us affectionately.

Relations with our 11th sign are often either friendly or patronizing; we treat them reverently, while they treat us with friendly condescension. Sometimes, these relationships develop in an 'older brother' or 'high-ranking friend' sense; indeed, older brothers and sisters are often our 11th sign. In terms of personal and sexual relationships, our 11th sign is always inclined to enslave us. This tendency is most clearly manifested in such alliances as Capricorn and Pisces or Leo and Libra. A child who is the 11th sign to their parents will achieve greater success than their parents, but this will only make the parents proud.

Our 2nd sign should bring us financial or other benefits; we receive a lot from them in both our business and our family life. In married couples, the 2nd sign usually looks after the financial situation for the benefit of the family. Sexual attraction is strong.

Our 6th sign is our 'slave'; we always benefit from working with them and it's very difficult for them to escape our influence. In the event of hostility, especially if they have provoked the conflict, they receive a powerful retaliatory strike. In personal relations, we can almost destroy them by making them dance to our tune. For example, if a husband doesn't allow his wife to work or there are other adverse family circumstances, she gradually becomes lost as an individual despite being surrounded by care. This is the best-case scenario; worse outcomes are possible. Our 6th sign has a strong sexual attraction to us because we are the fatal 8th sign for them; we cool down quickly, however, and often make all kinds of demands. If the relationship with our 6th sign is a long one, there is a danger that routine, boredom and stagnation will ultimately destroy the relationship. A child born under our 6th sign needs particularly careful handling as they can feel fear or embarrassment when communicating with us. Their health often needs increased attention and we should also remember that they are very different from us emotionally.

Finally, we turn to relations with our own sign. Scorpio with Scorpio and Cancer with Cancer get along well, but in most other cases, however, our own sign is of little interest to us as it has a similar energy. Sometimes, this relationship can develop as a rivalry, either in business or in love.

There is another interesting detail - we are often attracted to one particular sign. For example, a man's wife and mistress often have the same sign. If there is confrontation between the two, the stronger character displaces the weaker one. As an example, Prince Charles is a Scorpio, while both Princess Diana and Camilla Parker Bowles were born under the sign of Cancer. Camilla was the more assertive and became dominant.

Of course, in order to draw any definitive conclusions, we need an individually prepared horoscope, but the above always, one way or another, manifests itself.

Tatiana Borsch

Made in the USA
San Bernardino, CA
11 November 2019

59743519R00027